The Hairy Hamster Hunt

Tony Bradman is probably best known for his stories about **Dilly**, the world's naughtiest dinosaur. He has also edited many popular short story and poetry anthologies. **The Hairy Hamster Hunt** follows Tony's highly successful young poetry collection, entitled **Off to School,** also published by Macdonald Young Books.

Since he began in 1990, Chris Fisher has illustrated over 60 children's books. This is his first title for Macdonald Young Books.

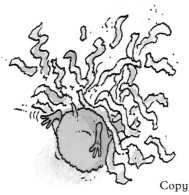

First published in Great Britain in 1999
by Macdonald Young Books,
an imprint of Wayland Publishers Ltd
61 Western Road
Hove
East Sussex
BN3 1JD

Copyright in this collection © Tony Bradman 1999
Illustrations copyright © Chris Fisher 1999

Find Macdonald Young Books on the internet at
http://www.myb.co.uk

Printed and bound by Proost International Book Co.

British Library Cataloguing in Publication Data available.

ISBN 0 7500 2663 4

THE
HAIRY HAMSTER
HUNT

Compiled by
TONY BRADMAN

AND OTHER
PET POEMS

Illustrated by
CHRIS FISHER

MACDONALD YOUNG BOOKS

In the Pet Shop

I think I'll have a tiger
or a wallaby… or three.
Or a red-kneed tarantula
or a fine and frisky flea.

Or a camel or a donkey –
the odd penguin or two?
Or perhaps I'll simply settle
for a kindly kangaroo.

I could have a tiny mole
or a vole – maybe a stoat,
a shiny shark, a crocodile
or a bearded nanny goat?

An octopus? A badger?
A giant squid? A guppy?
An orangutan? A vulture?
Or…
…what about that little puppy?

Michaela Morgan

Owner Wanted

Must be bouncy,
Good with sticks,
Think it's cruel to teach dogs tricks.

Must know teeth
Need bones to gnaw.
Must drop tit-bits
On the floor.

Must love puddles,
Muddy races.
Mustn't mind
A few chewed laces.

Must scratch ears
And hairy bellies.
But…
…Most of all…
…They must be SMELLY!

Judy Waite

Axolotl

Michael thought he'd found a bottle
Perfect for his axolotl.
But no matter how he tried
Percy would not fit inside.
The bottle neck was far too thin
To get an axolotl in.

So Michael kept him in the basin
The one his sister washed her face in.
When he heard her shout and scream
He found her looking sick and green.
She had cleaned her teeth that night
With axolotl and Ultrabrite.

So Michael took him off to school
And threw him in the swimming pool.
When you're swimming if you feel
Something chewing at your heel,
It's Percy telling you 'take care'
Not to squash him now he's there.

Frieda Hughes

Our Stick Insects

Our stick insects are a wonderful sight
Still in the daytime and still at night.
(They never move.)
Kept in a sweet jar, fed privet leaves,
They stand on our hands and crawl up our sleeves.
(We've trained them to do tricks.)
Mum goes bananas when we let them out
She freezes with fear and screams and shouts.
(We just call out 'Stay!' and they stay.)
She says she can cope with spiders but just can't bear
The thought of a stick insect in her hair.
(We told her that was bats but she didn't take any notice.)
She said the stick insects cannot stay
Not even for one more single day.
(What can you do?)
So we've brought them to school to give to friends
And that's where our pet stick insects' story ends.
(Well, more or less.)
We didn't actually give them away
So much as swap them for...

                  ...a tarantula.
(Can't wait to get home and show Mum...)

Irene Yates

Puppy Love

Fido's been sick on the carpet,
He's given the curtains a chew,
And the dining-room chairs
Are all covered in hairs
(And, by the back door, there's a poo).

I know that he's 'not just for Christmas' –
We've got him the rest of each year;
But I wish we had one
Who ate Pedigree Chum
Instead of my 'Notts Forest' gear.

Though nine out of ten prefer tinned foods,
We went and chose one who does not;
He's the sort of dog who
Gives my trainers a chew –
But he's still the best friend that I've got!

Trevor Harvey

Big Fat Budgie

I'm a big fat budgie.
I don't do a lot.
Might park on my perch.
Might peck in my pot.
Might peek at my mirror.
Might ring my bell.
Might peer through the bars of my fat budgie cell.
Might say 'Who's a pretty boy then?'
Might not.
I'm a big fat budgie.
I don't do a lot.

Michaela Morgan

Dead Ugly

Although I love our little cat,
She will leave offerings on the mat.
It started off with shrews and mice;
And then a baby hedgehog, twice.
The later gifts were hard to take:
A squashed-out frog, a blood-stained snake;
A squirrel that was rather stale;
A fox-cub with a missing tail.
But yesterday her special prize
Just made me gulp and rub my eyes;
I'd never seen a brute so big –
A Vietnamese pot-bellied pig!

John Yeoman

Out Walking

My doll's pram is special. It's full of cat-purr.
If you like, look inside. See that grey ball of fur?
It's wrapped round one ginger and two tabby kittens,
One brother, two sisters, and all with white mittens.

Today, for the first time, they opened their eyes
Like six blinking blueflakes from warm summer skies,
And sniffed at my fingers when I tickled their toes
With curious noses, each pink as a rose.

But now we're out walking. I'm pushing with care
This pram full of family enjoying the air.
And Minky, their mother, just opens one eye
Whenever we're stopped by friends passing by.

They peep in the pram and say, 'oh look how sweet!
How lucky you are to have such a treat!'
But who's getting the treat – me, pushing with pride?
Or Minky and babies, who are having the ride?

Catherine Benson

Bad Dog Translates

'Come here!'
Twitch an ear.

'Time for a walk!'
Jump and cavort.

'Get down!'
Yap and clown.

'Be quiet!'
Bark and riot.

'Sit and stay!'
Run away.

'Don't roll in that!'
Squash it flat.

'You reek!'
Lovely fragrance. Is it sheep?

'Bath time!'
Hide and whine.

'Don't bite the towel!'
Shake it and growl.

'Ugh! Your breath makes me feel sick!'
Cover me in sloppy licks.

'Leave the neighbour's cat alone!'
Chase that cat! Protect our home!

'What happened to that chicken leg?'
Look innocent. Be cute and beg.

'Bad dog! Bed! Get out of my sight!'
Sweet dreams, good dog, nighty night.

Jane Clarke

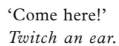

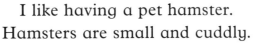

Pet Hamsters

I like having a pet hamster.
Hamsters are small and cuddly.
They are sweet and fluffy.
They have round bright eyes.
They disappear in the paper shavings and you think they've run away.
I snuggle mine and talk to it.
I feed it and stroke it.
But even so, I do love it when they die.

Sorry little hamster.

But then I can build a teeny tiny coffin: brill!
And I can make a little wooden cross: lush!
And I have to bury it and be really sad: great!

I love having a pet hamster.

Rebecca Lisle

The Memory Place

Down the bottom of the garden
At the back of the shed
Is the place we always bury
Our pets when they are dead.

There's a gerbil called Blackeye,
The hamsters Fred and Fritz,
The guinea pig called Goldie
Which my sister loved to bits.

A mouse or two, the budgie
Grandma taught to give three cheers,
And Abigail, the old grey cat
We'd had for years and years.

It ought to be a sad place
But that really isn't so.
A place to think, to dream, just be?
That's the place we go.

Patricia Leighton

Purring

When my cat sleeps
    Curled up in a ball,
You can't really see
    Her head at all.

A furry circle
    Curled around,
Sleeping softly
    With a purring sound.

She looks funny,
    Does our cat,
Like a furry,
    Purring hat.

I'd like to wear her
    On my head,
Or have her warm
    My toes in bed.

And when you touch her
    Curled and warm,
Her purring purrs
    All up your arm.

But then she hears
    A sudden sound
And she's no longer
    Curled around.

She's not sleeping,
    Softly there…
She's gone – but left
    Some purring air…

Tony Bradman

Meems

Other cats purr
and so does Meems.

Other cats creep
and so does Meems.

Other cats sleep
and so does Meems,

But Meems
dreams.

She dreams of moths with velvet wings.
She dreams of prawns (her favourite things).
She dreams of windows striped with rain
and dipping her nose in a puddle again.

Other cats miaow, other cats snore,
other cats lie in a slope on the floor
but Meems

dreams.

Adèle Geras

Vet's Surgery

Yap and squawk and yowl and growl,
grunt and oink, miaow,
flap and balk and howl and scowl.
Who brought in that cow?

Treated toad for diarrhoea.
Plastered bone.
Stitched rat's ripped ear.
Bandaged badger's poorly paw.
Soothed a horse's saddle sore.
Gave the kiss of life to fish.
Shampooed hamster – ticklish.
Sold worm tablets for a worm.
Poked a pig to kill a germ.
Put a pigeon's wing in splints.
Cured a cockatoo of squints.
Showed a wallaby with bumps
How to balance when she jumps.

Yap and squawk and yowl and growl,
grunt and oink, miaow,
flap and balk and howl and scowl.
Who brought in that cow!

Gina Douthwaite

I Love Little Pussy

I love little pussy,
    Her coat is so warm,
And if I don't hurt her
    She'll do me no harm.
So I'll not pull her tail,
    Nor drive her away,
But pussy and I
    Very gently will play.
She shall sit by my side,
    And I'll give her some food;
And pussy will love me
    Because I am good.

ANON

Ruddles And His Periscope

Our ginger cat moves like a submarine
through a sea of tall grass,
stalking a bird or a mouse it has seen
flash like a looking-glass,
sending a signal to each of its kind –
look out! that old tom is not far behind!

Gingerly, cautiously, silent as smoke,
he slinks up on his prey.
We know any second he'll pounce at a stroke,
it's all part of his play.
As much as we all admire his skill
we can't let him win or home in for the kill.

We whistle. His tigery-tail – once
limp as a skipping-rope –
suddenly stiffens and pokes through the
grass like a steel periscope.
He looks over the field and knows it to be
time to surrender and slink home for tea.

Edward Storey

The Pet

My mum gave me some money
   To buy myself a treat;
She said I could buy anything
   (As long as it wasn't sweets).

So off I went to spend it.
   I wandered round the shops;
I couldn't find a thing to buy…
   …Then something made me stop.

There in a pet shop window
   I saw a flash of fire;
I saw some scales and burning eyes
   And I knew my heart's desire.

I gave the man my money.
   He handed me a lead.
Then I walked out of the pet shop
   With the only pet I need.

A pet with wings and gleaming fangs,
 With skin that's shiny green;
With claws, and a tail that's longer
 Than any tail you've seen.

 A pet whose breath is orange flame,
 Whose ears both hiss with steam,
Who'll fly me to the land of clouds,
 And to the land of dreams.

 But first I'd better go home.
 I hope that it's OK...
 I hope my mum will like my pet.
 I wonder what she'll say?

 Tony Bradman

Snakes Are Slithery

Snakes are slithery,
Snakes are fun.
Mine's a friendly,
Harmless one.
Snakes are beautiful,
Snakes are cool,
But teachers don't like
Snakes in school.
(I can't imagine why.)

His favourite food
Is slug and snail.
Wriggly tadpoles
Never fail.
I gather them,
When they're in season.
(Mum won't help,
For some strange reason.)

Don't be frightened,
He's no harm.
Watch him curling
Up your arm.
Hear the hissing
Sound he makes.
(I can't understand
Why you don't like snakes.)

Malachy Doyle

Goldie

Goldie the guinea-pig
lives in a hutch.
She sits and she sniffles
but she doesn't do much.
I give her food and water.
I change her straw.
But most of all, I love her.
That's what she's for.

Tony Mitton

The Hairy Hamster Hunt

I've looked on the table
I've searched through the fridge;
the cheese box is empty,
I've felt in each vase!
I've checked under carpets,
beneath the settee,
behind every cushion,
below the TV…

Yes, I'm sure that I closed it,
honestly Dad –
I knew if I didn't
you'd really be mad!
YES, I know he was safe
when I last saw him, Mum…
Well, I think that I'm sure…
Yes, I'm sure that I am!

That is…
I'm sure he'll soon come…
LOOK OUT!
DON'T STEP BACK, MUM!

Judith Nicholls

Missing Rabbit

My rabbit's lost,
I'm sad to say.
She's left her hutch
And gone away.

We searched through every
Inch of ground.
But poor old Scamp
Could not be found.

I wrote upon
A piece of board:
RABBIT MISSING –
SMALL REWARD.

HER NAME IS SCAMP
SHE'S WHITE AND BLACK.
AND I WOULD REALLY
LIKE HER BACK.

I tied it to
The garden gate
And now can only
Sit and wait.

Barry On

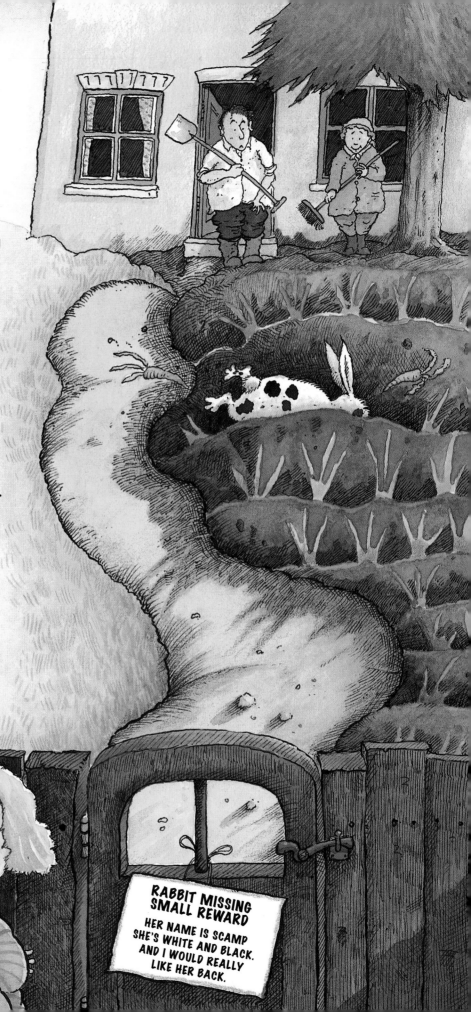

RABBIT MISSING
SMALL REWARD
HER NAME IS SCAMP
SHE'S WHITE AND BLACK.
AND I WOULD REALLY
LIKE HER BACK.

Fudge

Fat as a cloud
and paler than toffee,
marked with a swirl
like cream in coffee,
apple addict, carrot muncher,
sawdust sleeper, midnight walker,

squeak of a wheel in the heart of the night,
creak of a cage door that swings in the moonlight.

Who made holes in my duvet cover?
Who chewed through the phone wires?
Who stole Polos from my brother
and wheeled them under the gas fire?

Patter of claws on the kitchen work surface
whisper of whiskers searching the fridge,

nut nibbler, cornflake cruncher,
apple addict, carrot muncher,

cool as cream
stirred into coffee,
down cracks in floorboards
he stretched like toffee,
food fiend, freedom finder,
fear-nothing feast forager,
nut nobbler, night nibbler,
fat as a ball of butter –
Fudge.

Helen Dunmore

Little Hairy Harry

Little hairy Harry is the opposite of horrible
Little hairy Harry is a real ace dog.

I don't need alarm clocks
To get me out of bed
My dog Harry comes and snuffles round my head.
When it's time to wake up
I don't need a shout –
My dog Harry comes to *love* me out.

A cold wet nose like a friendly slug,
A warm wet tongue, and a face to hug,
He'd like to get in with me all cosy and snug,
But my mum would go berserk – and I'm no mug,
So I fall out of my duvet and we wrestle on the rug.

When I've got the miseries –
Rain and thunder in my heart –
Harry sits so close to me you can't split us apart.
He doesn't ask me 'What's up?'
He doesn't ask 'Why?'
He just *loves* the sun back into my sad sky.

A cold wet nose like a friendly slug,
Wild bushy eyebrows like a spider or a bug,
A warm wet tongue, and a face to hug,
Paws dead dirty from holes he's dug.
If he wants you then he'll get you. He'll just tug, tug, tug.

Little hairy Harry is the opposite of horrible.
Happy hairy Harry is my cool, ace dog.

Jan Dean and Christopher Lees

Wet Pets

Fish are easy.
Fish don't talk.
They don't need taking
For a walk.

They don't leave hairs.
They never roam
Or eat you out of
House and home.

If they get moods
They never show it.
If they wee,
You'd never know it.

They don't do much
Apart from swim.
You give them names
Like Jaws and Jim.

Sometimes I sit
And watch them bubble.
Get a wet pet.
They are no trouble.

Kaye Umansky

Tony Bradman and Macdonald Young Books
would like to thank the following for
contributing to this collection:

In the Pet Shop © Michaela Morgan 1999

Owner Wanted © Judy Waite 1999

Axolotl © Frieda Hughes 1999

Our Stick Insects © Irene Yates 1999

Puppy Love © Trevor Harvey 1999

Big Fat Budgie © Michaela Morgan 1999

Dead Ugly © John Yeoman 1999

Out Walking © Catherine Benson 1999

Bad Dog Translates © Jane Clarke 1999

Pet Hamsters © Rebecca Lisle 1999

The Memory Place © Patricia Leighton 1999

Purring © Tony Bradman 1999

Meems © Adèle Geras 1999

Vet's Surgery © Gina Douthwaithe 1999

I Love Little Pussy © Anon.

Ruddles And His Periscope © Edward Storey 1999

The Pet © Tony Bradman 1999

Snakes Are Slithery © Malachy Doyle 1999

Goldie © Tony Mitton 1999

The Hairy Hamster Hunt © Judith Nicholls 1999

Missing Rabbit © Barry On 1999

Fudge © Helen Dunmore 1999

Little Hairy Harry © Jan Dean and Christopher Lees 1999

Wet Pets © Kaye Umansky 1999

For more information about
poetry titles published by
Macdonald Young Books,
contact: *The Sales Department,
Macdonald Young Books,
61 Western Road, Hove,
East Sussex BN3 1JD.*